h dissolutions, to cause others to be elected; whereby the Legislative Powers, in

e exposed to all the dangers of invasion from without,

turalization of Foreigners; refusing to pass others to enc

stice, by refusing his Assent to Laws for establishing Judiciary Powers

ir salaries. —— He has erected a multitude of New Offices, and sent hith

Standing Armies without the Consent of our legislatures. —— He has affec

us to a jurisdiction foreign to our constitution, and unacknowledged by our

g us: — For protecting them, by a mock Trial, from Punishment for any

arts of the world: — For imposing Taxes on us without our Consent: —

tended offences. —— For abolishing the free System of English Laws in a n

e an example and fit instrument for introducing the same absolute rule i

ally the Forms of our Governments: — For suspending our own Legislatur

Government here, by declaring us out of his Protection and waging War agains

He is at this time transporting large Armies of foreign Mercenaries to compleat

he most barbarous ages, and totally unworthy the Head of a civilized nation. —

e the executioners of their friends and Brethren, or to fall themselves by their Ha

tiers, the merciless Indian Savages, whose known rule of warfare, is an undistin

edress in the most humble terms: Our repeated Petitions have been answered only by re

of a free people. Nor have We been wanting in attentions to our British br

us. We have reminded them of the circumstances of our emigration and settlem

mon kindred to disavow these usurpations, which, would inevitably interru

e must, therefore, acquiesce in the necessity, which denounces our Separation,

ore, the Representatives of the united States of America, in Gen

ame, and by authority of the good People of these Colonies, solemnly Publish an

re Absolved from all Allegiance to the British Crown, and that all political co

Independent States, they have full Power to levy War, conclude Peace, contra

apable of Annihilation, have returned to the People at large for their exercise

__ He has endeavoured to prevent the Population of these States; for t

their, and raising the conditions of new Appropriations of Lands. ___ Th

He has made Judges dependent on his Will alone, for the tenure of their off

swarms of Officers to harrass our People, and eat out their substance ___ H

to render the Military independent of and superior to the Civil power. ___

aws; giving his Assent to their Acts of pretended Legislation: ___ For quarter

urders which they should commit on the Inhabitants of these States: ___

For depriving us in many cases, of the benefits of Trial by Jury: ___ For tr

ghbouring Province, establishing therein an Arbitrary government, and enla

to these Colonies: ___ For taking away our Charters, abolishing our most

, and declaring themselves invested with power to legislate for us in all c

us. ___ He has plundered our seas, ravaged our Coasts, burnt our towns, an

he works of death, desolation and tyranny, already begun with circumstances of

__ He has constrained our fellow Citizens taken Captive on the high Seas t

ds. ___ He has excited domestic insurrections amongst us, and has endeav

ished destruction of all ages, sexes and conditions. In every stage of thes

cited injury. A Prince, whose character is thus marked by every act which m

thren. We have warned them from time to time of attempts by their legislature to

t here. We have appealed to their native justice and magnanimity, and we h

t our connections and correspondence. They too have been deaf to the voice

nd hold them, as we hold the rest of mankind, Enemies in War, in Peace Fr

al Congress, Assembled, appealing to the Supreme Judge of the world for th

declare, That these United Colonies are, and of Right ought to be Free a

nection between them and the State of Great Britain, is and ought to be tota

Alliances, establish Commerce, and to do all other Acts and Things which

Chief Justice John Marshall

by Charles M. & Margaret K. Wetterer
Illustrated by Kurt W. C. Walters

Prologue

"If American Law were to be represented by a single figure, skeptic and worshipper alike would agree that the figure could be one alone, and that one, John Marshall."

—Oliver Wendell Holmes

It was January, 1801. The chief justice of the United States Supreme Court, Oliver Ellsworth, had resigned. President John Adams had lost the November election that would have given him a second term as president. Adams, a member of the Federalist party, wanted to appoint a new chief justice before the newly elected president Thomas Jefferson, a member of the Republican party, took office in March and appointed one himself. Adams's choice was John Jay. Jay had been the first chief justice, but had resigned in 1795 to become governor of New York. Jay declined the appointment. Like most leaders of the time, he did not want the job of chief justice because he believed the Supreme Court was not, and would never be, an influential part of the United States government.

President Adams turned to his secretary of state, John Marshall, and asked, "Whom shall I nominate now?" Secretary Marshall suggested several names, but Adams rejected them all. Finally, the president sighed and said, "I believe I must nominate you." John Marshall accepted at once. Over the next 34 years, under Chief Justice Marshall's leadership, the Supreme Court became an increasingly effective branch of the government, equal in power and influence to that of the president and the legislature.

Many years later, someone asked John Adams what he thought was his most important accomplishment as president. Without hesitation, Adams replied, "My appointment of John Marshall as chief justice."

John Marshall was born on September 24, 1755, in a two-room log cabin near Germantown, on the western frontier of what was then the British colony of Virginia. He was the first of 15 children born to Thomas and Mary Marshall.

John was just a toddler when his parents started giving him chores around the house. As he grew, his mother taught him how to read and write. His father showed him how to farm, hunt, fish, and ride a horse. Then, when John was ten years old, Thomas Marshall moved his growing family to a larger house he built in a densely forested area. Here John fished the streams and shot game in the woods surrounding his home to help feed the family.

Like most frontier children of the time, John worked hard and played hard, too. He and his brothers and sisters played ball, ran races, shot marbles, and played quoits. Quoits—a game of ring toss much like horseshoes—was a favorite game, and John was good at it.

QUOITS
Two pegs or stakes were set in the ground about 19 yards (17.4 m) apart. A player stood by one peg and pitched his quoit, a ring of rope or flattened metal about eight inches (20.3 cm) in diameter, to the far peg. The goal, as in horseshoes, was to encircle the peg or to get as close to the peg as possible.

The Marshall family greatly enjoyed the all-too-rare visitors to their home. George Washington was an especially welcome guest. Washington and John Marshall's father had been friends since childhood. As young men, Washington and Thomas Marshall had worked surveying, or mapping land, together. They explored western Virginia, marked boundaries, and drew up detailed maps. Over the years, on his visits to the Marshall home, George Washington and young John Marshall grew to know and like each other.

When Marshall was 14 years old, his parents sent him to a small school in Westmoreland County, more than 100 miles (161 km) from home. Here, at the Reverend Archibald Campbell's academy, John studied Latin, history, logic, and literature. Not only was he a good student, he also excelled in sports. He was a champion in quoits. John met and became a good friend of schoolmate James Monroe, who would, many years later, become the fifth president of the United States.

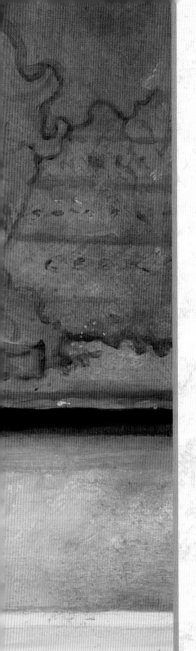

In 1770, after just one year at the school, John returned home to help run the family farm. A young minister, Reverend James Thomson, who lived for a time in the Marshall's home, tutored John and the older children for the next year. When Reverend Thomson left, John continued to study on his own. In 1772, John's father bought a set of law books. John discovered he enjoyed the subject, and before long, he was spending every spare minute studying law. As his interest in the law grew, he decided he would become a lawyer. His determination was so strong, in fact, that he would walk almost 20 miles (32 km) to borrow books and discuss the law with a lawyer friend of his father.

Around that time, 17-year-old John and his younger brothers helped their father build a seven-room frame house ten miles (16 km) away in Fauquier County. They called their new home Oak Hill. Theirs was the first home in the area with real glass windows. John's mother was proud of this touch of luxury. Glass windows were uncommon at this time because glass was both expensive and difficult to transport.

This was a time of increased prosperity and ambition for the Marshalls and most colonists. However, it was also a time of growing discontent with the British, who ruled the colonies from across the ocean, in faraway England. In December 1773, colonists in Massachusetts, disguised as Native Americans, dumped a shipment of tea into Boston Harbor to protest the British tax on tea. Colonial newspapers gleefully referred to the event as The Boston Tea Party. The British reaction to this challenge to their governing power was to send more soldiers to enforce the tax laws . . . which just made things worse.

By 1774 the Marshalls and many other settlers throughout the 13 colonies were becoming more and more outspoken in their protests against unfair British laws. These laws had been made by the British Parliament in England, where the colonists had no one to speak for them and no vote on matters affecting them. They resented British restrictions on their ability to trade with other countries and the limitations placed on what goods they could manufacture. They detested the British laws that limited their political freedom. Most of all they hated being so heavily taxed.

In response to the growing unrest, some 50 delegates from the American colonies met in Philadelphia in September 1774 to form the First Continental Congress. The delegates decided to act together to appeal to Britain for justice. In the name of all the colonies, they created and delivered a petition to King George III of Great Britain that was called the Declaration of Rights and Grievances. In London the British Parliament rejected the petition and sent even more troops over to enforce their despised laws.

Meanwhile, Patrick Henry, a prominent lawyer and a member of the Virginia colonial legislature, spoke out against the British oppression. "Is life so dear, or peace so sweet, as to be purchased at the price of chains and slavery? Forbid it, Almighty God! I know not what course others may take; but as for me, give me liberty or give me death."

Colonists everywhere took up Patrick Henry's cry. The Red Coats, as British soldiers were called because of the long red coats that were part of their uniform, fought with colonists at Lexington and Concord, Massachusetts. News of these first battles for independence traveled fast. Men began forming local militias, or small armies, that they called Minutemen. They were ready to fight at a moment's notice. Marshall's father helped to form the local regiment in Fauquier County, Virginia, and 19-year-old John Marshall joined. When the officer of Marshall's company failed to show up for training, John was made a lieutenant and put in charge in his place. Marshall quickly read all the books he could find on military training. Throughout the spring and hot summer, Marshall drilled his volunteers on how to be effective fighters. Often he would end the training session by organizing a game of quoits.

In May 1775, a Second Continental Congress in Philadelphia appointed George Washington as Commander in Chief and commissioned him to organize a Continental Army that would draw men from all 13 colonies. In the fall of that year, John's company was ordered to Williamsburg, Virginia, to help drive out the British troops. A few miles from Norfolk, Virginia, they met a British regiment and fought a short and bitter battle. The Minutemen cheered as the Red Coats retreated and scrambled aboard their ships in Norfolk Harbor. Before sailing away, however, the British ships bombarded the city with heavy cannon fire. John and his men watched helplessly as Norfolk burned to the ground. By this time, all hope of a peaceful settlement between the colonists and Britain had gone up in smoke.

The Declaration of Independence

In June 1776, representatives from the 13 colonies met in Philadelphia. They decided to dissolve all political connections between the colonies and Britain. Thomas Jefferson, a prominent lawyer and delegate to the Continental Congress, prepared a draft of a document declaring the colonies' independence. After a few minor changes, this declaration was unanimously agreed upon.

The delegates met again in Philadelphia on July 4, 1776, and signed the Declaration of Independence. In part, the document stated "... That these United Colonies are, and of Right ought to be Free and Independent States; that they are Absolved from all Allegiance to the British Crown, and that all political connection between them and the State of Great Britain, is and ought to be totally dissolved." The Revolutionary War had officially begun.

After the first public reading of the Declaration of Independence on July 8, 1776, the great bell of the Philadelphia State House rang out to proclaim the colonies' freedom. This bell was thereafter called the Liberty Bell.

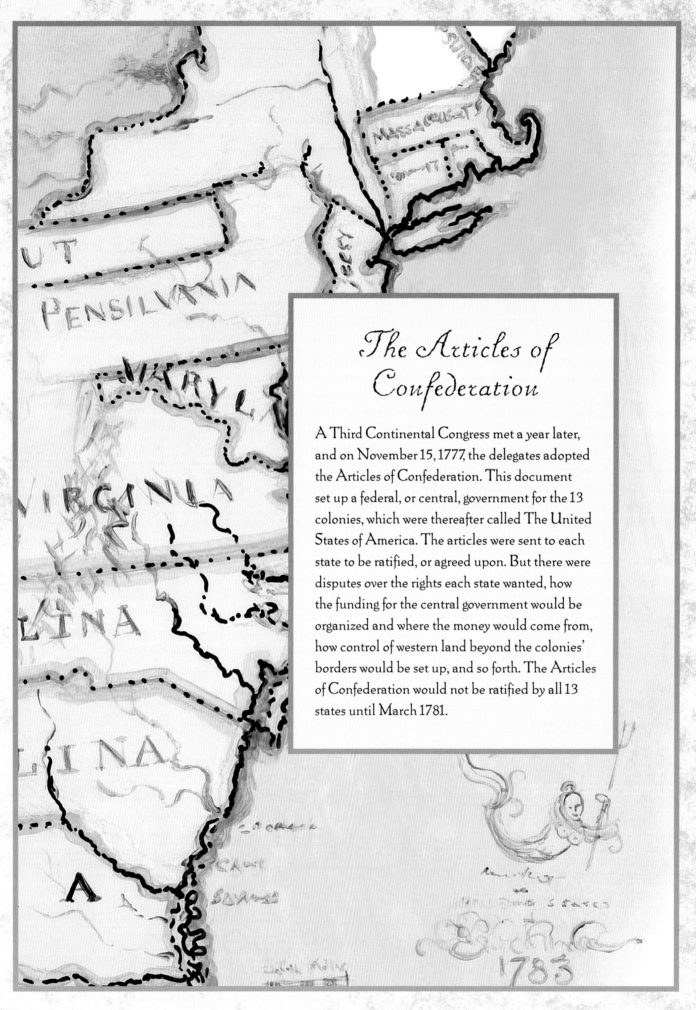

The Articles of Confederation

A Third Continental Congress met a year later, and on November 15, 1777, the delegates adopted the Articles of Confederation. This document set up a federal, or central, government for the 13 colonies, which were thereafter called The United States of America. The articles were sent to each state to be ratified, or agreed upon. But there were disputes over the rights each state wanted, how the funding for the central government would be organized and where the money would come from, how control of western land beyond the colonies' borders would be set up, and so forth. The Articles of Confederation would not be ratified by all 13 states until March 1781.

In 1776, John Marshall joined and was commissioned as a first lieutenant in General George Washington's Continental Army. He served in Virginia, New Jersey, New York, and Pennsylvania. Marshall was one of the 12,000 men who suffered with Washington during the deadly cold winter of 1777–1778 as they camped at Valley Forge, Pennsylvania. Washington appointed Marshall to be a deputy judge advocate. His job was to settle disputes among the war-weary soldiers. The men soon recognized Marshall as a fair and intelligent judge. He grasped issues quickly and was just in his decisions. Marshall was promoted to captain in 1779 and sent to Yorktown, Virginia, to await orders for a new assignment.

In Yorktown at the time was Marshall's father, a colonel commanding his own regiment. Next to his headquarters lived Colonel Jaquelin Ambler, his wife Rebecca Ambler, and their four daughters. When Colonel Marshall mentioned to the Amblers that his son was coming to Yorktown, the girls were thrilled at the possibility of meeting the eligible bachelor. In late December 1779, 24-year-old John Marshall finally arrived. He was tall, skinny, and awkward. The Ambler sisters were disappointed—all but 14-year-old Mary, who was known to all as Polly. She liked Marshall's brown eyes, curly black hair, and shy manner. And he was completely charmed by pretty, dark-haired Polly. He loved her bright and cheerful sense of humor. They quickly discovered they enjoyed each other's company . . . very much.

While he awaited his next assignment, John began a law course at William and Mary College in nearby Williamsburg, Virginia. He visited Polly often. But two months later, Colonel Ambler was transferred to Richmond, Virginia, and his family went with him. Marshall did not want to risk losing Polly, so he left school and followed her.

While in Richmond, Marshall applied for a license to practice law. He returned to Fauquier County, his official residence, to be sworn in as an attorney. The following year, after having served six years, Marshall resigned from the Army and opened a law office. He then ran for the Virginia House of Delegates from Fauquier County and was elected. During this time, he traveled back and forth between Fauquier County and Richmond as often as he could to court Polly.

One day someone told Marshall that Polly had another serious suitor. Marshall dropped everything, rode to Richmond, and asked Polly to marry him. When Polly hesitated, he thought she meant no. Sick at heart, Marshall mounted his horse and rode away. "John! John!" Polly cried after him. But he was gone. She ran to her father and, weeping, begged him to ride after Marshall to tell him that her answer was "Yes!"

On January 3, 1783, Polly Ambler, not quite 17, and 27-year-old John Marshall were married. During this same year, Britain finally recognized the American colonies' independence, and the Liberty Bell rang out again with the joyful news.

John and Polly Marshall lived contentedly in Richmond, where he practiced law. Marshall was an intelligent, hardworking, and effective lawyer. Within just a few years, he had become a leading attorney in Richmond. Once when a farmer came to town looking for the best lawyer to handle his legal problem, everyone he asked suggested he talk to Marshall. Then someone pointed Marshall out to him. The farmer took one look at this shabbily dressed fellow, strolling along eating berries he had gathered in his hat, and decided he would prefer a more successful-looking lawyer. Later however, as the farmer waited in court for his case to be called, he witnessed his smart-looking, well-dressed attorney lose a case to Marshall. He fired his lawyer at once and begged Marshall to take his case. He had only five dollars left after paying off the first attorney, but when the farmer told Marshall the story, Marshall laughed, accepted the money, and won the case.

The Constitution

In the years following independence, it became increasingly clear that the Articles of Confederation —the document that bound the 13 states into a single country—were not working effectively. The states treated each other as if they were foreign countries rather than parts of single, unified country. The Continental Congress called a convention in May 1787. They decided to change the Articles of Confederation and write a constitution for the United States.

Delegates to the Continental Congress generally supported one of two ideas for the organization of the government of the United States. Some, including George Washington and John Adams, wanted a strong central, or federal, government that would run the entire country. They were called Federalists—one of the two main political parties of the time. Others, like Thomas Jefferson and Patrick Henry, believed in strong individual state governments that would cooperate in running the country. They were known as Antifederalists or Republicans. At the convention in Philadelphia, Federalists and Republicans worked together to write the Constitution of the United States.

In order for the new constitution to become law, two thirds, or nine of the 13 states, had to ratify it. Marshall wanted Virginia to ratify the new constitution. For this reason he ran for and was elected to the Virginia legislature for a third time.

Virginia's Constitutional Convention met in June 1788. Patrick Henry spoke out against ratification. As a champion of states' rights, he did not want a strong central government controlling the future of Virginia. Marshall, however, argued that only a strong central government could keep the states together as one unified country. Marshall helped convince Virginia's convention delegates to vote in favor of ratification of the constitution.

Finally by 1789, nine states had ratified the new constitution, and it became law. George Washington was elected as the first president of the United States. Washington offered Marshall various government jobs, but he turned them all down. Marshall wanted to be home with Polly and their growing family. Eventually John and Polly Marshall would have a total of ten children, six of whom—five boys and one girl—would live to adulthood.

The X, Y, Z Affair

The Revolutionary War did not end the problems the United States had with Britain. President Washington, however, believed that the young country could not fight and win another war so soon after the fight for independence. Reluctantly he agreed to a treaty that gave the British several special trade advantages. Many Americans were disappointed. They felt that the United States was giving up too much to Britain in order to secure peace. And the French, who were at war with the British, were furious because they felt the United States was helping England. When John Adams was elected president, he sent Marshall and two other envoys to try to improve relations between the United States and France.

When Marshall and his fellow envoys arrived in France after the long voyage across the Atlantic, the French foreign minister refused even to see them. Instead, three French agents met with the envoys and demanded, among other things, a bribe of $250,000. Marshall wrote to President Adams describing the attempted bribe and his absolute refusal to pay. Marshall's letters did not name the three French agents—he called them X, Y, and Z. In the letters he detailed the repeated failures to reach any agreement with the French. Finally, Marshall gave up and sailed for America. While he was on the long voyage home, American newspapers published the letters Marshall had sent to President Adams.

When Marshall landed in New York in June 1798, he felt he had failed. Instead the public hailed him as a national hero. Americans admired Marshall's honesty and courage in dealing with the French agents. As he rode to the capital, cheering crowds lined the streets.

Not long after his return from France, Marshall's old friend George Washington urged him to run for Congress. Marshall decided to do so and was elected. Then, in May 1800, the president at the time, John Adams, asked Marshall to become secretary of state, one of the most important jobs in the executive, or presidential, branch of the government. Marshall accepted the position and had served less than a year when Supreme Court Chief Justice Oliver Ellsworth resigned and President Adams offered Marshall the job. Without hesitation, he agreed. In January 1801, the Senate unanimously confirmed John Marshall's appointment as the fourth chief justice of the United States.

The Supreme Court

The Founding Fathers created the Supreme Court to rule on federal and state legal cases involving the United States or the Constitution. Treaties, controversies affecting the nation, conflicts between two or more states or citizens of different states, and cases including public officials may all be heard by the Supreme Court. Most often the Court hears appeals about decisions made by lower federal courts and from the highest state courts in cases involving a national or constitutional question. All federal and state courts must accept and follow decisions handed down by the United States Supreme Court.

Congress has always decided the number of judges who are on the United States Supreme Court. When the Supreme Court was established in 1789, it had six justices. Since 1869, there have been nine justices. Judges who sit on the Supreme Court are selected by the president and must then be approved by a majority vote of the Senate.

The authors of the Constitution had intended the Supreme Court, the third or judicial branch of the government, to be equal in authority to the president and Congress. However, in the early years of the nation, it had not worked out that way. In fact, the Supreme Court had very little power. The court had no way to enforce its decisions on its own, and a president, if he chose, could simply refuse to have the decisions of the court enforced at all—rendering the time and effort invested in making these decisions pointless.

Congress, if they thought about the Supreme Court at all, considered it of little importance in national affairs. In its early days, the Supreme Court didn't even have a courtroom in which to hold sessions. At first, the court met in a local tavern. By the time Marshall became chief justice, the Supreme Court was meeting in a basement room beneath the Senate building in Washington.

During Marshall's tenure as chief justice, the power, prestige, and influence of the Supreme Court gradually grew. The wise and far-reaching decisions of the court both strengthened the country's union and protected citizens' civil rights.

Landmark Cases

❧ One of the Marshall court's early decisions, a case called *Marbury v. Madison (1803)*, made it clear that the Supreme Court had the authority to declare that a law passed by Congress was unconstitutional. That meant that if the law went against what was written in the Constitution, the court could declare the law invalid, or not legal. This power of the Supreme Court, called judicial review, was one of the most important in the court's history because it established the court's authority to reject laws that undermine the Constitution.

❧ Another case, *Fletcher v. Peck (1810)*, made it clear that the Supreme Court also had the ability to declare state laws unconstitutional. The *Fletcher v. Peck* decision kept a state from interfering with an individual's rights regarding personal property without good reason.

❧ The decision in the case of *Dartmouth College v. Woodward (1819)* established that a valid contract signed in one state must be respected by all states. And the ruling in the *McCulloch v. Maryland (1819)* case gave Congress the power to make laws about subjects that are not specifically mentioned in the constitution, but are instead implied, or hinted at. This implied power has given Congress the ability to continue to operate as conditions change within the country and the world.

❧ The case of *Gibbons v. Ogden (1824)* gave the federal government control over interstate commerce (business between states). This decision insured that states would work together instead of against each other.

Under Marshall's leadership, the Supreme Court gradually became the influential and respected third branch of the government it was intended to be, equal in importance to the executive (the office of the president) and legislative (the Congress) branches. Chief Justice Marshall's decisions helped bring the once separate states that had become the United States closer together. As a result, the nation was strengthened. Without Chief Justice Marshall and the Supreme Court decisions on these and other cases, the Constitution as we know it might not have survived.

As chief justice, Marshall's name became well known, but people did not always recognize him. Sometimes his clothes were so worn and ragged that he looked more like an unemployed laborer. Once while he was waiting for Polly outside a general store in Richmond, a man came out, handed Marshall a box of groceries, and told him to take it to his carriage. Marshall carried the groceries and, with a nod and a smile, accepted a coin for his service.

While the Supreme Court was in session in Washington, Marshall lived at a nearby boarding house. Here he was just as informal in manner and dress as he was at his home in Richmond. People of all ages and classes felt at ease with him. Once a lawyer brought his young son to the boarding house to meet the chief justice. Marshall, seeing how shy and uncomfortable the youngster was, challenged the boy to a game of marbles. Off they went to the backyard, where they were soon on their hands and knees playing marbles in the dirt. While it was not an uncommon sight to see Marshall playing marbles with young boys—his own and others, quoits was always his favorite pastime. Marshall even organized the Quoits Club of Richmond in 1788 and remained a member for the rest of his life.

John Marshall's life-long love, his "dearest Polly," had never been a robust person. With the birth of each child (remember, there were ten of them), and as she grew older, her health declined. On December 24, 1831, as Marshall sat beside her sickbed, Polly lovingly hung around his neck a locket containing a strand of her hair. The next day she died. Polly was 65 years old. "I have lost her," Marshall cried, "and with her have lost the solace of my life." Marshall continued to serve as chief justice, but much of his joy in living died along with Polly. Less than four years later, on July 6, 1835, John Marshall died. He was wearing Polly's locket.

A grateful nation mourned John Marshall, who had served as chief justice of the United States for over 34 years. In Philadelphia, the Liberty Bell that had rung out in 1776 to proclaim the new nation's independence now rang in memory of Chief Justice John Marshall. As the bell tolled to mark his passing, it cracked. The Liberty Bell never rang again.

John Marshall was laid to rest beside his beloved Polly. He left to the American people a strong Supreme Court whose decisions would frame the conscience of the nation and define the law of the land. Many people who study American history agree that John Marshall was our greatest chief justice.

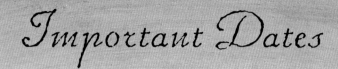

Important Dates

September 24, 1755—John Marshall was born in Virginia

1769—Attended boarding school for one year

1775—Enlists in local militia

July 4, 1776—Declaration of Independence signed

1776—Commissioned a lieutenant in Continental Army

1777–1778—With Washington at Valley Forge

December 1779—Meets Mary Willis Ambler, known as Polly

August 28, 1780—Sworn in as an attorney

1781—Leaves Army and opens law practice

1782—Elected to Virginia House of Delegates

January 3, 1783—Marries Polly Ambler

1788—Persuades Virginia convention delegates to vote for ratification
of Constitution

1789—George Washington becomes first president of United States

1797—Marshall appointed envoy to France

1798—Hailed as national hero in XYZ Affair

1799—Elected to United States Congress

1800—Becomes John Adams's Secretary of State

1801–1835—Serves as the fourth Chief Justice of the United States

1803—*Marbury v. Madison*

1810—*Fletcher v. Peck*

1819—*Dartmouth College v. Woodward*

1819—*McCulloch v. Maryland*

1824—*Gibbons v. Ogden*

December 25, 1831—Polly Ambler Marshall dies

July 6, 1835—Chief Justice John Marshall dies and
the Liberty Bell tolls for the last time

For our brothers and sisters
—C.M.W. and M.K.W.

For information contact:
MONDO Publishing
980 Avenue of the Americas
New York, NY 10018

Visit our website at www.mondopub.com

Printed in China

07 08 09 10 11 12 HC 9 8 7 6 5 4 3 2 1
09 10 11 12 PB 9 8 7 6 5 4 3 2

ISBN (HC) 1-59336-306-0
ISBN (PB) 1-59336-307-9

Book Design by Edward Miller

Library of Congress Cataloging-in-Publication Data

Wetterer, Charles M.
     Chief justice / by Charles M. & Margaret K. Wetterer ; illustrated by Kurt K.C. Walters.
        p. cm.
     Summary: Profiles John Marshall, who was appointed chief justice of the Supreme Court by
President John Adams in 1801 and served for thirty-four years, a time in which the Court became
as powerful and influential as the other branches of government.
     ISBN 1-59336-306-0 (hardcover) — ISBN 1-59336-307-9 (pbk.)
        1. Marshall, John, 1755-1835. 2. United States. Supreme Court—Biography—Juvenile literature.
3. Judges—United States—Biography—Juvenile literature. 4. Judges—Selection and appointment—
United States—History— Juvenile literature. [1. Marshall, John, 1755-1835. 2. Judges. 3. United
States. Supreme Court—Biography.] I. Wetterer, Margaret K. II. Walters, Kurt W. C., 1963- ill. III. Title.

KF8745.M3W48 2005
347.73'2643—dc22
[B]

2003065194

pable of Annihilation, have returned to the People at large for their exercise

—— He has endeavoured to prevent the Population of these States; for th

their, and raising the conditions of new Appropriations of Lands. ——

He has made Judges dependent on his Will alone, for the tenure of their off

swarms of Officers to harrass our People, and eat out their substance ——

to render the Military independent of and superior to the Civil power. ——

laws; giving his Assent to their Acts of pretended Legislation: —— For Quarter

Murders which they should commit on the Inhabitants of these States: ——

For depriving us in many cases, of the benefits of Trial by Jury; —— For tra

Neighbouring Province, establishing therein an Arbitrary government, and enla

to these Colonies: —— For taking away our Charters, abolishing our most

and declaring themselves invested with power to legislate for us in all c

us. —— He has plundered our seas, ravaged our Coasts, burnt our towns, and

the works of death, desolation and tyranny, already begun with circumstances of

—— He has constrained our fellow Citizens taken Captive on the high Seas to

—— He has excited domestic insurrections amongst us, and has endeavo

distinguished destruction of all ages, sexes and conditions. In every stage of these

repeated injury. A Prince, whose character is thus marked by every act which m

thren. We have warned them from time to time of attempts by their legislature to e

here. We have appealed to their native justice and magnanimity, and we h

our connections and correspondence. They too have been deaf to the voice

hold them, as we hold the rest of mankind, Enemies in War, in Peace Fri

Congress, Assembled, appealing to the Supreme Judge of the world for the

declare, That these United Colonies are, and of Right ought to be Free an

nection between them and the State of Great Britain, is and ought to be totall

Alliances, establish Commerce, and to do all other Acts and Things which

the Protection of divine Providence, we mutually pledge to each other